The Little Pigs' First Cookbook

by N. Cameron Watson

Little, Brown and Company
Boston Toronto

for my idol
Wendy

First Edition

Library of Congress Cataloging-in-Publication Data
Watson, N. Cameron (Nancy Cameron)
The little pigs' first cookbook.

Summary: Three pig brothers share simple, healthy recipes that very young cooks can prepare for breakfast, lunch, and dinner.
1. Cookery—Juvenile literature. [1. Cookery]
I. Title.
TX652.5.W365 1986 641.5'123 85-23833
ISBN 0-316-92467-9

Designed by Trisha Hanlon

Published simultaneously in Canada
by Little, Brown & Company (Canada) Limited

DNP

Printed in Japan

This little pig had a rub-a-dub,
This little pig had a scrub-a-scrub,
This little pig-a-wig ran upstairs,
This little pig-a-wig called out, Bears!
Down came the jar with a loud Slam! Slam!
And this little pig had all the jam.

Table of Contents

This is Charles.

This is Bertram.

This is Ralph.

They are brothers, and they are just learning how to cook.

Charles gets up early. He turns the radio on and sings along while he cooks breakfast.

“Breakfast is ready!” he calls up the stairs.

The three brothers sit down to eat. Bertram hopes Ralph will cheer up soon. Ralph is rather grumpy because he just this minute woke up.

It only takes three bites to make everyone happy again. This is because breakfast comes from Charles's Breakfast Menu.

Charles's

Breakfast Menu

Charles's Yum-lish Yogurt

Breakfast Cereal

Boozled Eggs

Toast *Français*

Personal Pancakes

Charles's Yum-lish Yogurt

This serves 1 pig.

1. **Spoon** about ½ cup plain yogurt into a breakfast bowl.

2. **Stir in** 1 tablespoon golden raisins
   a sprinkle of cinnamon

3. **Cut up and add** *(Make sure you cut with the knife pointing away from you.)*
   ¼ banana
   ¼ peach
   10 grapes
   4 orange sections

4. **Stir** if desired.

Charles prefers his unstirred.

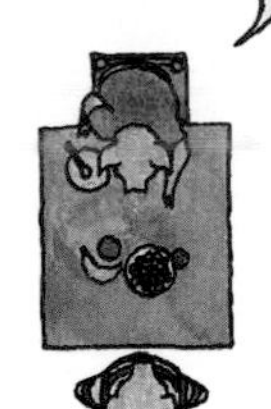

Can I please have some more?

But this is supposed to be enough for 1 little pig!

Other ideas:

- For __________ 's YUM-LISH YOGURT, use your own favorite combination of fruits.
- For CHARLES'S CRUMB-LISH YOGURT, sprinkle some breakfast cereal over the top.
- For CHARLES'S HUM-LISH YOGURT, hum as you make it.

Yogurt's great when you're in a hurry!

Higglety, pigglety, pop!
The dog has eaten the mop;
The pig's in a hurry,
The cat's in a flurry,
Higglety, pigglety, pop!

Breakfast Cereal

This makes about 2 quarts. That is the same as 8 cups.

1. **Preheat** oven to 325° F.
2. **Chop** 2 cups walnuts
3. **Mix**
   4 cups rolled oats
   1 cup wheat germ
   ½ cup sesame seeds
   ½ cup millet
   the chopped walnuts
4. **Heat and add**
   ¾ cup honey
   ¼ cup oil
   ½ teaspoon salt
   2 teaspoons vanilla extract
   Heat this mixture over low heat until it is thin enough to mix in well with the dry ingredients.
5. **Spread** thinly and evenly on cookie sheets.
6. **Bake** in preheated oven, stirring occasionally. REMOVE when golden brown. COOL.
7. **Add** 2 cups raisins
8. **Serve** in a bowl with cold milk. Add fresh fruit if desired.

If one serving is ½ cup, how many servings will one batch make?

Ask someone to help you with the oven.

Chew each bite thoroughly to get the full flavor.

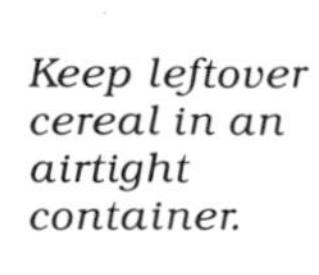

Keep leftover cereal in an airtight container.

Boozled Eggs

Make 1 egg for each small pig or 2 for each big pig.

There are 8 tablespoons in a stick of butter.

Eggs hatch only if they have been fertilized.

1. **Break**	1 egg into a bowl. Do not beat it.
2. **Add**	1 tiny pinch salt 1 tiny pinch nutmeg*
3. **Melt**	½ tablespoon butter in a small skillet over low heat.
4. **Pour**	egg into skillet. Break and stir egg quickly with a fork. Keep the heat low—have you ever tasted eggs that have become browned?
5. **Continue**	stirring with the fork as you cook until egg is just barely set. This will take only about 30 seconds.
6. **Serve**	on a warm plate.

**Or use your favorite spice or herb, such as:*
mint
chives
rosemary
thyme
tarragon
sage
oregano
dill
cumin
pepper
paprika

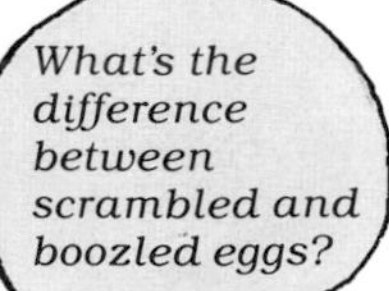

Higgety, piggety, my black hen
She lays eggs for gentlemen;
Gentlemen come every day
To see what my black hen doth lay.

Toast Français

Make 1 slice for each serving.

How do you say "toast" in French?

"Toast" with a French accent.

French toast is actually an American dish.

What are some other French cooking words?

Hmm . . . "sauté" means fried . . . "le pain" is bread . . . "le beurre" is butter . . . and "un oeuf" is an egg.

1.	**Whisk**	1 egg ¼ cup milk ½ teaspoon vanilla extract ¼ teaspoon ground cinnamon
2.	**Pour**	egg mixture into a flat pan.
3.	**Soak**	2 slices dry bread in mixture until soggy, about 5 minutes.
4.	**Melt**	1 tablespoon butter in a skillet over low heat.
5.	**Place**	bread in hot skillet.
6.	**Fry**	until golden brown.
7.	**Turn**	slices over carefully with a spatula. Add more butter for the other side if pan is dry.
8.	**Fry**	until golden brown on other side.
9.	**Serve**	hot with butter and maple syrup.

Ralph, Bertram, and I fell out,
And what do you think it was all about?
They love coffee and I love tea,
And that was the reason we couldn't agree.

Personal Pancakes

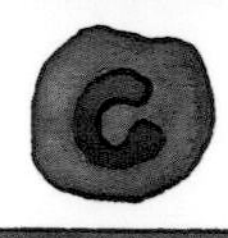  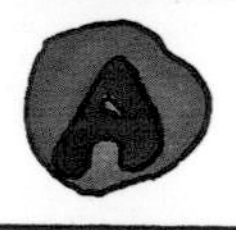    

This usually serves 4, but when Ralph is hungry, it serves only him!

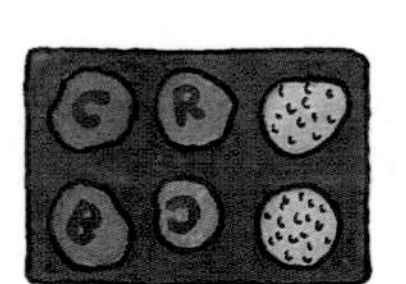

You may use a griddle instead.

1.	**Sift**	1 cup flour 1 teaspoon baking powder ½ teaspoon salt Mix in a bowl.
2.	**Whisk**	1 egg ⅔ cup milk 2 tablespoons melted butter Mix in another bowl.
3.	**Stir**	the two mixtures together in ten strokes until just mixed.
4.	**Melt**	½ tablespoon butter in a hot skillet. Dribble in some of the pancake batter to form your initials backwards in the skillet. Cook 20 seconds, then cover the letters with batter to form a pancake.
5.	**Fry**	until you see bubbles on surface.
6.	**Turn; then fry**	until other side is golden brown.
7.	**Continue**	making pancakes until batter is used up.
8.	**Serve**	hot with butter and maple syrup.

Hold your initials up to a mirror to see what they look like backwards.

What does A look like backwards?

Use a soup spoon for the letters and a ladle for the pancakes.

Mix a pancake
Stir a pancake
Pop it in the pan;
Fry the pancake,
Toss the pancake—
Catch it if you can!

After breakfast, Charles goes outside. He has decided to build a fort. Ralph resumes work on a story he is writing on the computer.

Bertram returns his books to the library. He browses for some time, looking for new books to take home. He finds a number of interesting storybooks, a book about insects, and a new book on mathematical games.

Soon it is eleven o'clock. Bertram quickly checks out his books and runs back to the house. It is time to start lunch.

What should he make? It is a difficult decision. Everything is so good when it's from Bertram's Lunch Menu.

Bertram's
Lunch Menu

Bertram's Blushing Pigs

Guinea Pig Salad

Tomato Alphabet Soup

Grilled Geometric Sandwiches

Devilish Eggs

Bertram's Blushing Pigs

Use 1 tomato for each pig.

Herb suggestions:
basil
mint
chives
parsley
thyme

Cut off the very tip of the carrot to make the snout flat.

1. **Cut** 1 ripe tomato in half horizontally. Scoop insides out of bottom half.
2. **Mix** ¼ cup cottage cheese
   1 teaspoon chopped fresh herb
3. **Fill** the tomato half with the cheese mixture. Put upside down on a plate.
4. **Cut** the stem end off 1 cherry tomato. Place flat side down on plate next to pig's body. This will be the head.
5. **Peel** 1 small carrot. Cut off small end to use for snout. Cut rest of carrot into sticks for the arms and legs.
6. **Cut** holes in blushing pig's face for carrot snout and raisin eyes to fit into. Add ears made from tomato scraps.

Sometimes I like to put clothes on my blushing pigs: lettuce skirts, sliced cheese trousers, cucumber hats, and peanut buttons.

There was a lady loved a swine,
Honey, quoth she,
Pig-hog, wilt thou be mine?
Hough, quoth he.

Guinea Pig Salad

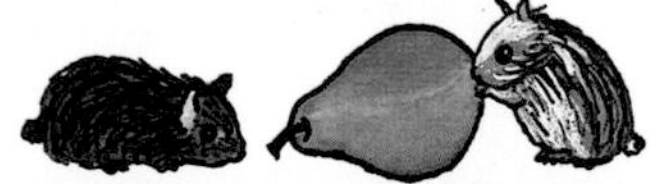

One pear serves 2 little pigs.

This is a nice lunch for a hot day.

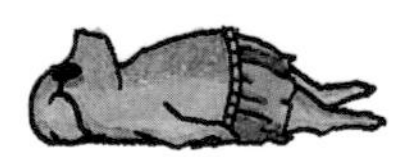

1. **Peel**	1 fresh ripe pear Use canned pears if you can't find nice fresh ones.
2. **Cut**	the pear in half lengthwise. Scoop out the core.
3. **Place**	1 lettuce leaf on each of two small plates.
4. **Grate**	a 1-inch cube of cheddar cheese onto each leaf. This makes beds of "straw."
5. **Place**	1 pear half, round side up, on each bed of cheese.
6. **Place**	a mound of cottage cheese at big end of pear for tail.
7. **Decorate**	the small end of the pear with raisins for eyes and nose. Use sliced almonds for ears.

Use a little cottage cheese for a little tail or a lot for a big tail.

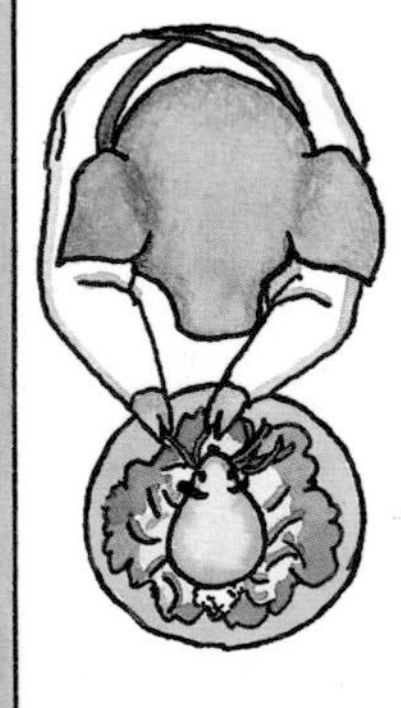

If your guinea pig wants whiskers, use carrot peels or thin strips of cheese.

There was a little guinea pig,
Who being little was not big;
He always walked upon his feet,
And never fasted when he eat.

Tomato Alphabet Soup

A B C D E F G H I J K L M N
O P Q R S T U V W X Y Z

This makes enough for 3 BIG pigs!

1. **Chop** 1 peeled medium-sized onion
   3 medium-sized ripe tomatoes
   2 celery sticks
2. **Melt** 1 tablespoon butter in a large, heavy saucepan.
3. **Sauté** the onions and celery in the butter over low heat until soft.
4. **Add** the tomatoes and simmer until soft. Stir often so they won't stick.
5. **Add** ¼ cup dried alphabet noodles
   2½ cups milk
6. **Heat** slowly until noodles are tender. Do not let soup boil, or it will curdle!
7. **Serve** in bowls or cups. Can you find your initials?

Onions grow underground.

"Sauté" is a French word. It comes from "sauter," meaning to cook quickly in fat.

Great A, little a,
Bouncing B,
The cat's in the cupboard
And can't see me.

Grilled Geometric Sandwiches

Here are some other fillings you can use: peanut butter and honey; cream cheese and raisins; tuna fish.

This recipe makes 1 sandwich.

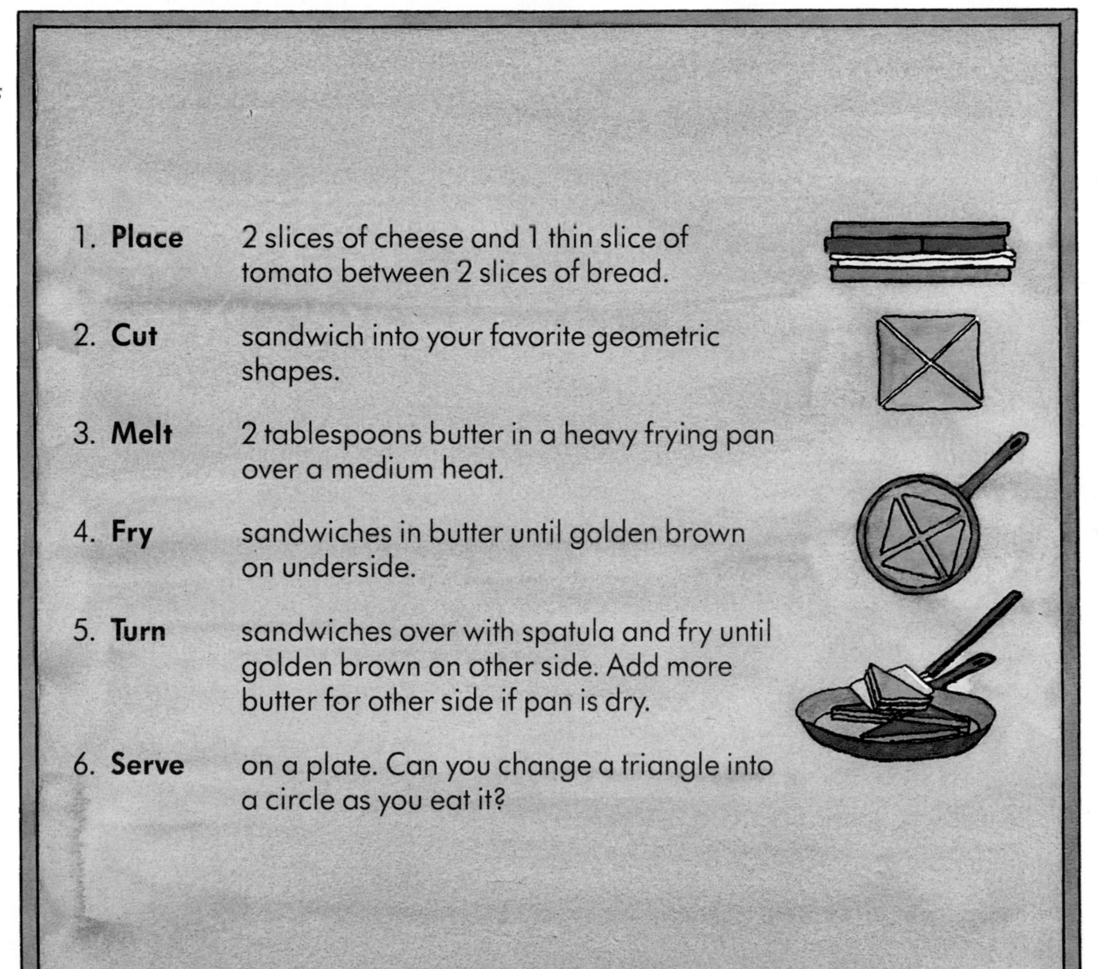

1. **Place** 2 slices of cheese and 1 thin slice of tomato between 2 slices of bread.
2. **Cut** sandwich into your favorite geometric shapes.
3. **Melt** 2 tablespoons butter in a heavy frying pan over a medium heat.
4. **Fry** sandwiches in butter until golden brown on underside.
5. **Turn** sandwiches over with spatula and fry until golden brown on other side. Add more butter for other side if pan is dry.
6. **Serve** on a plate. Can you change a triangle into a circle as you eat it?

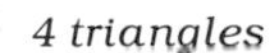

4 triangles

1 circle and 1 odd shape

2 rectangles

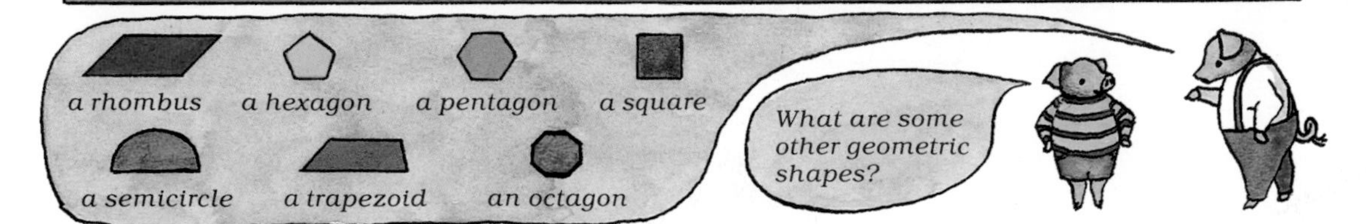

Devilish Eggs

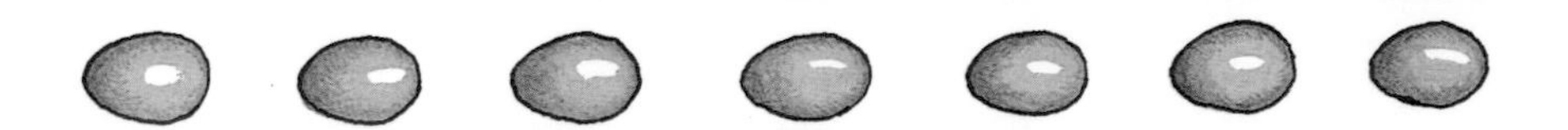

Each egg serves 1 little pig. Use 2 each for big pigs!

These are called Devilish Eggs because they usually taste hot and spicy. Add a few drops of Tabasco to the yolks if you like them spicy.

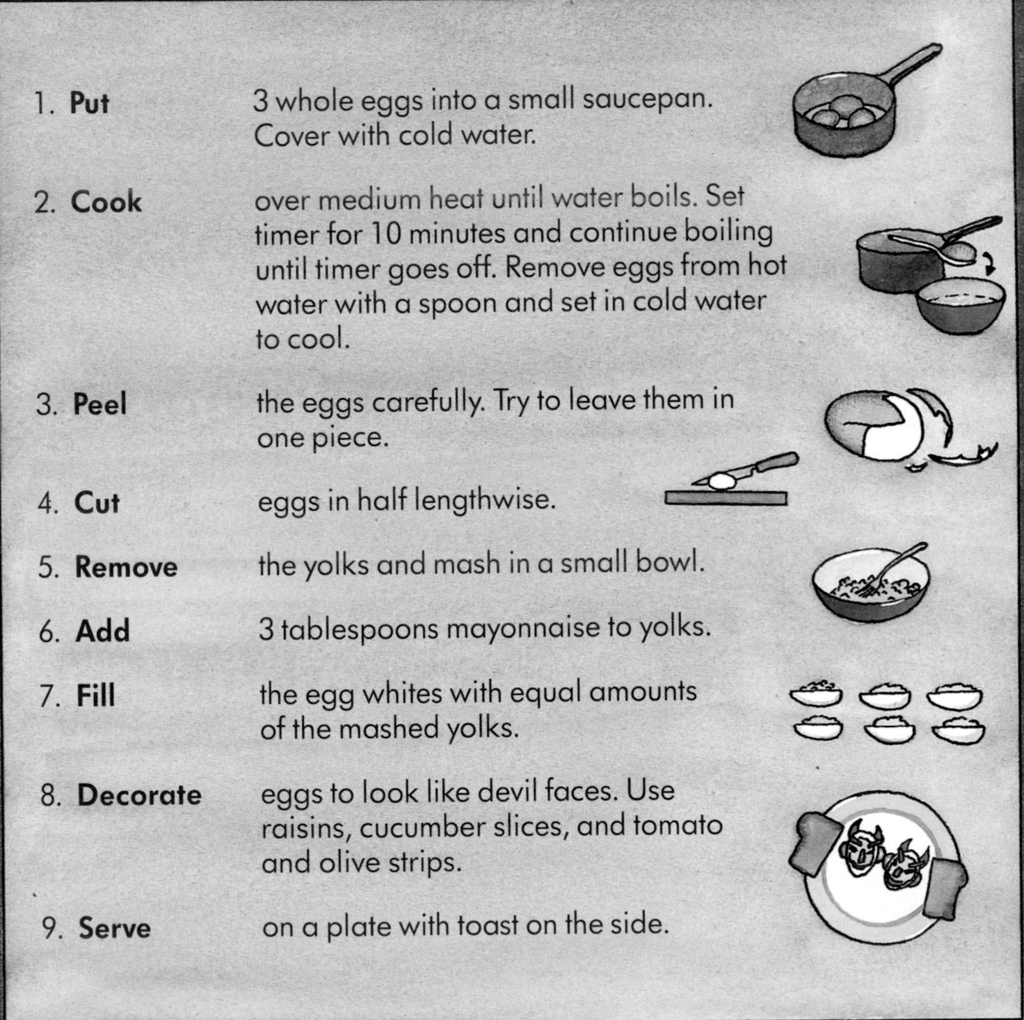

1. **Put** 3 whole eggs into a small saucepan. Cover with cold water.
2. **Cook** over medium heat until water boils. Set timer for 10 minutes and continue boiling until timer goes off. Remove eggs from hot water with a spoon and set in cold water to cool.
3. **Peel** the eggs carefully. Try to leave them in one piece.
4. **Cut** eggs in half lengthwise.
5. **Remove** the yolks and mash in a small bowl.
6. **Add** 3 tablespoons mayonnaise to yolks.
7. **Fill** the egg whites with equal amounts of the mashed yolks.
8. **Decorate** eggs to look like devil faces. Use raisins, cucumber slices, and tomato and olive strips.
9. **Serve** on a plate with toast on the side.

St. Dunstan, as the story goes,
Once pulled the devil by his nose
With red-hot tongs, which made him roar,
That could be heard ten miles or more.

Lunch is over.

"Let's play tag!" says Charles. Bertram would rather play Scrabble, but Charles insists.

Ralph is tempted to join them, but instead he goes for a long walk. He wants to think about things.

Ralph is late getting home and starting dinner, but he works quickly. Soon everything is ready.

Here are the delicious things from Ralph's Dinner Menu.

Ralph's

Dinner Menu

Ralph's Own Pizza

Seashell Melt

Piglet's Popovers

Maple Baked Beans and...

...Boston Brown Bread

Ralph's Own Pizza

This makes 4 little pizzas. I get 2 and the others each get 1!

1.	**Preheat**	oven to 400° F.
2.	**Chop**	1 large peeled onion 2 large ripe tomatoes
3.	**Add**	¼ teaspoon each thyme, oregano, and basil
4.	**Crush**	2 cloves garlic; add to tomatoes.
5.	**Melt**	1 tablespoon butter in a heavy skillet.
6.	**Sauté**	all ingredients in butter until sauce is thick. Stir often. If you let sauce stick to the bottom of the pan, it will burn.
7.	**Split**	2 pieces pita bread. Place the 4 rounds on a large baking sheet.
8.	**Spread**	sauce over each bread round.
9.	**Grate**	6 ounces mozzarella cheese
10.	**Sprinkle**	cheese over rounds.
11.	**Bake**	in preheated oven until cheese is golden and bubbly (approximately 10 minutes).
12.	**Serve**	at once!

Pizza is great with a green salad or sliced green peppers.

If you like your pizza sauce as RICH as I do, add twice as much garlic!

If cheese gets too brown, it does not taste good.

Come, let's to bed,
Says Sleepy-head;
Tarry a while, says Slow.
Put on the pot,
Says Greedy-gut,
We'll sup before we go.

Seashell Melt

Serve with lots of vegetables or a nice big salad.

This makes enough for 3 or 4 little pigs.

1. **Preheat** oven to 400° F.
2. **Boil** 2 quarts of slightly salted water in a large pot.
3. **Add** 2 cups shell noodles and cook about 15 minutes.
4. **Drain** noodles. Put into a 1-quart casserole and set aside.
5. **Melt** 2 tablespoons butter in a heavy saucepan.
6. **Add** 1 small chopped onion
   1 tablespoon flour
   Cook until onion is soft.
7. **Add** 1½ cups of milk. Whisk until smooth.
8. **Grate** 3 ounces cheddar cheese. Whisk ¾ of it into sauce.
9. **Pour** sauce over shells.
10. **Sprinkle** rest of cheese over top.
11. **Bake** in preheated oven until cheese melts, about 10 minutes.
12. **Grate** nutmeg over top of each serving.

The sauce is the ocean, the shells are the shells, and the nutmeg is the sand.

Nutmeg tastes much better when it is freshly ground.

She sells
Seashells
by the
Seashore

Try saying this poem, fast, three times in a row!

Piglet's Popovers

   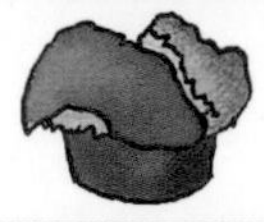  

This makes 6 popovers—enough for 6 little pigs, 3 big pigs, or 2 big pigs and 2 little pigs.

Serve with a crunchy cucumber and red pepper salad.

1. **Preheat** oven to 450° F.
2. **Butter** a 6-hole muffin tin.
3. **Whisk** 1 egg
   ½ cup milk
   1 tablespoon melted butter
   ½ cup flour
   Whisk together in a bowl until very smooth.
4. **Divide** batter evenly among the 6 muffin holes.
5. **Put** into preheated oven. Turn oven down to 375° F. Bake until dark golden brown, about 40 minutes.
6. **Boil** 6 eggs for 4 minutes just before popovers are done. Water should be boiling before you add the eggs.
7. **Cut** the top off each popover.
8. **Break** the eggshells and spoon insides of one egg into each popover.
9. **Sprinkle** 1 tablespoon grated cheese over each egg. Use your own favorite kind of cheese. Replace tops on popovers.
10. **Serve** while still warm!

It's the eggs that make popovers POP.

I can get a little time in on the computer while the popovers bake.

Rumpty-iddity, row, row, row,
If I had a good supper,
I could eat it now.

Maple Baked Beans and...

This makes about 1½ quarts, or enough for about 4 meals for 3 pigs. (That makes 12 servings.)

1. **Soak** 1 pound soldier beans in water overnight.
2. **Drain** beans. Cover with fresh water.
3. **Boil** until the skins pop when you blow on them. This will take about 20 minutes.
4. **Drain** the beans
5. **Put** the beans into a 2-quart earthenware bean pot, or use a heavy iron pot with a lid.
6. **Add** 2 cups water
   ½ cup maple syrup or honey
   4 tablespoons melted butter
   1 teaspoon dry mustard
   ¼ teaspoon pepper
   2 teaspoons salt

7. **Pour** mixture over beans.
8. **Peel and cut** 1 onion into quarters. Put on top of beans.
9. **Cover** the pot and bake at 250° F until beans are tender, about 5 to 6 hours. Add more water before and during baking if level of water drops below beans.

I like making these because it doesn't take long to mix them up. Then they can cook all day by themselves!

These get better every day. Just heat them as you need them.

They only take a few minutes to heat up at dinnertime.

Soldier beans come from Maine. They are very creamy and delicious, but if you can't find any, use pea beans instead.

...Boston Brown Bread

This makes 1 medium-large loaf of bread, or about 12 thick slices.

**These grains are best if coarsely ground. You can order them at the health food store.*

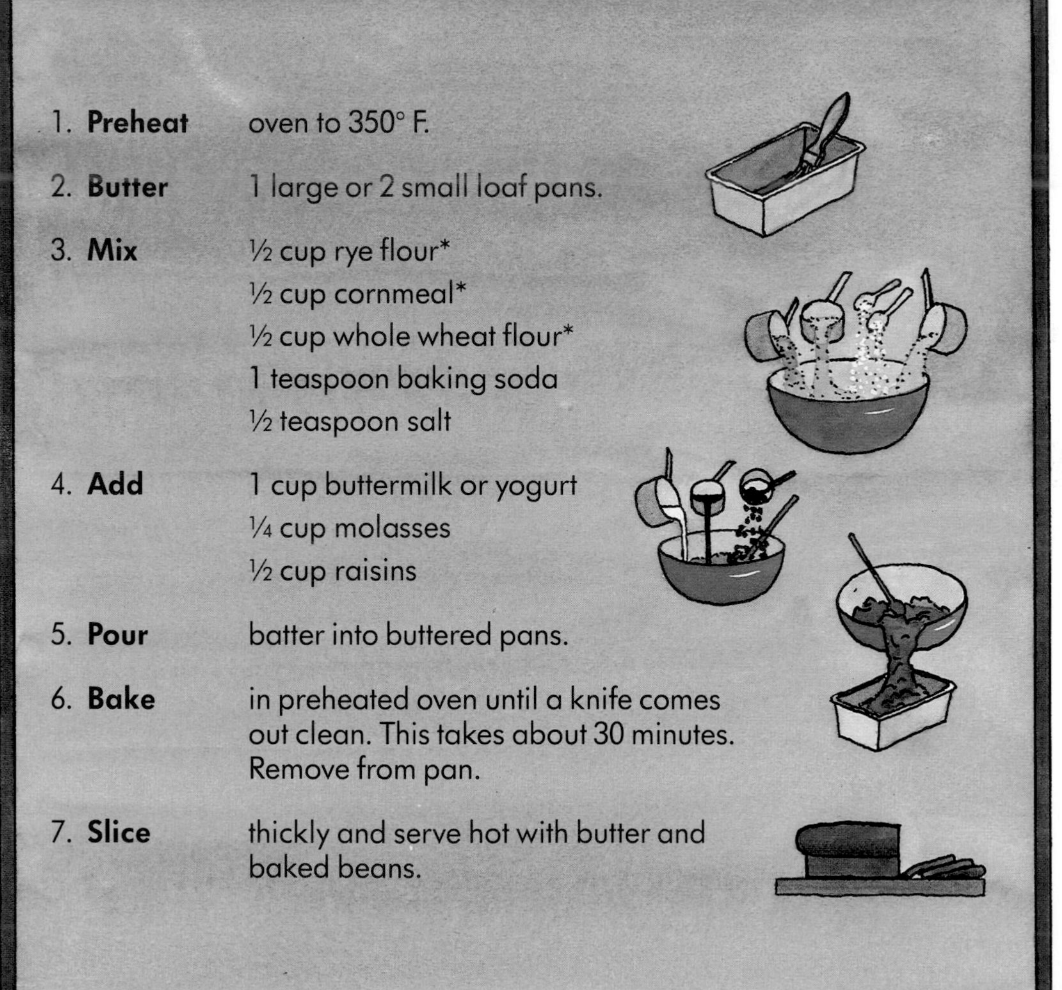

1. **Preheat** oven to 350° F.
2. **Butter** 1 large or 2 small loaf pans.
3. **Mix**
   ½ cup rye flour*
   ½ cup cornmeal*
   ½ cup whole wheat flour*
   1 teaspoon baking soda
   ½ teaspoon salt
4. **Add**
   1 cup buttermilk or yogurt
   ¼ cup molasses
   ½ cup raisins
5. **Pour** batter into buttered pans.
6. **Bake** in preheated oven until a knife comes out clean. This takes about 30 minutes. Remove from pan.
7. **Slice** thickly and serve hot with butter and baked beans.

When you eat this bread with baked beans, you get the same complete protein that you get from meats.

Blow, wind, blow!
And go, mill, go!
That the miller may grind his corn;
That the baker may take it,
And into bread make it,
And bring us a loaf in the morn.

One might imagine that the three brothers would be too full for dessert after all this good food, but they are not. After all, they are growing piglets.

Each one has a favorite sweet to put on The Pigs' Dessert Menu.

The Pigs'
Dessert Menu

Charles's Apple Smack

Bertram's Corner Cakes

Ralph's Bumptious Bananas

Charles's Apple Smack

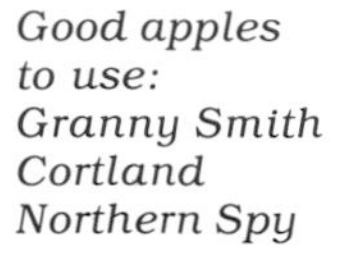

Good apples to use:
Granny Smith
Cortland
Northern Spy

1. **Preheat** oven to 350° F.
2. **Core and slice** 5 washed tart apples

3. **Add** juice and grated rind of 1 lemon
4. **Put** apples in an 8-by-8-inch baking dish.
5. **Mix** ¼ cup honey
   ¼ cup melted butter
   ½ teaspoon cinnamon

6. **Add** 1½ cups fresh whole wheat bread crumbs
7. **Spread** mixture over apples.
8. **Bake** in preheated oven until the top is golden brown and apples are tender (approximately 35 minutes).
9. **Serve** after it has cooled with a tall glass of milk.

The peels add color, flavor, and lots of vitamins!

My favorite combination is McIntosh and Red Delicious.

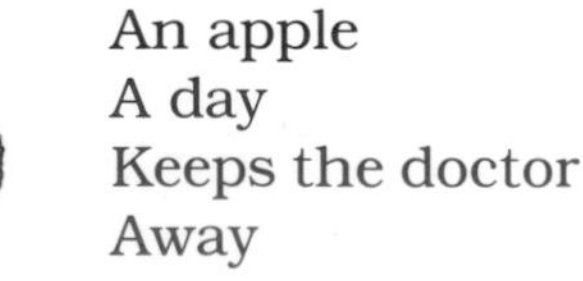

An apple
A day
Keeps the doctor
Away

Bertram's Corner Cakes

This makes about 12 Corner Cakes.

1. **Preheat** oven to 350° F.
2. **Butter** a 7-by-10-inch baking pan and set aside.
3. **Melt** ¼ cup butter in a large saucepan.
4. **Add** ½ cup honey
   ½ cup peanut butter
   1 egg
   1 teaspoon vanilla extract
   Whisk until smooth.
5. **Add** ¼ cup whole wheat flour
6. **Pour** batter into the prepared pan.
7. **Bake** in preheated oven about 20 minutes, or until a knife comes out clean.
8. **Cut** into squares. Each square is now a Corner Cake.
9. **Cool** Corner Cakes before serving. These keep well if covered tightly.

Peanut butter has lots of protein in it. You can make it by crushing peanuts with a mortar and pestle or in a food grinder.

With one Corner Cake you have 4 corners. . . .

If you cut it in half crossways, you would have 8 corners. . . .

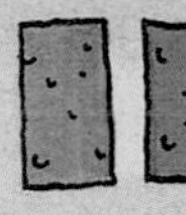

And if you cut it in half diagonally, you would have 6 corners!

Pat-a-cake, pat-a-cake, baker's man,
Bake me a cake as fast as you can.
Pat it and prick it, and mark it with "P,"
And put it in the oven for Piggy and me.

Ralph's Bumptious Bananas

Three bananas make enough for 3 pigs.

1. **Preheat** oven to 350° F.
2. **Melt** 3 tablespoons butter in a heavy 7-by-10-inch baking dish.
3. **Peel** 3 bananas
4. **Slice** in half lengthwise.
5. **Place** banana slices, flat side down, in the baking dish.
6. **Dribble** 3 teaspoons honey and 6 teaspoons lemon juice over the bananas.
7. **Bake** in preheated oven until bubbly, about 10 minutes.
8. **Place** 2 banana slices on each of 3 serving plates.
9. **Scrape** the juice from the baking dish over the bananas.
10. **Serve** while still warm.

The riper the bananas are, the sweeter they get.

This is the best, most scrumptious, bumptious dessert ever!

For a special treat, but only *very occasionally, serve with vanilla ice cream.*

Dickery, dickery, dare,
The pig flew up in the air;
The man in brown
Soon brought him down,
Dickery, dickery, dare.

Dessert is over and the kitchen cleaned up. Charles yawns. “Good night,” he says as he hugs his brothers.

Presently Bertram looks at the clock. "It's my bedtime," he says. He marks his place and closes his book.

Ralph stays up alone to work a little longer on his story. It is coming along nicely. Finally he, too, gets sleepy. He turns off the computer, switches the lights out, and goes to bed.

To Veryan
With love from Mummy and Daddy
for passing your first ballet exam
and being highly commended.

December 1989.